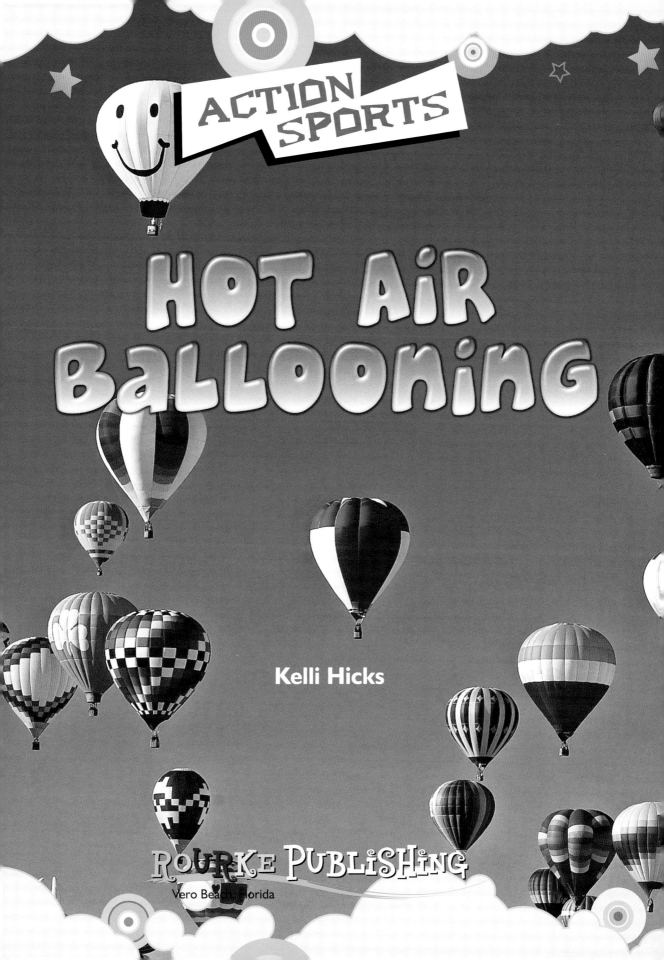

ACTION SPORTS

HOT AiR BALLOONiNG

Kelli Hicks

ROURKE PUBLISHING
Vero Beach, Florida

www.rourkepublishing.com

PHOTO CREDITS: Title Page ©BenC; Page 2-3 ©pasphotography; Page 5 ©Karen Gentry; Page 7 Library of Congress; Page 8 ©paul prescott; Page 9 Public Domain/Wiki; Page 10-11 ©BenC; Page 12 ©Razumovskaya Marina Nikolaevna; Page 13 ©Benjaminet; Page 14 ©Jakez; Page 15 ©Carlos Caetano; Page 16 ©Adrian Hughes; Page 17 ©Thomas Barrat; Page 18 ©Jonathan Lenz; Page 19 ©pasphotography; Page 21 ©Svetlana Tikhonova

Edited by Jeanne Sturm

Cover and Interior designed by Tara Raymo

Library of Congress Cataloging-in-Publication Data

Hicks, Kelli.
  Hot air ballooning / Kelli Hicks.
    p. cm. -- (Action sports)
  Includes index.
  ISBN 978-1-60694-358-8
  1. Hot air balloons--Juvenile literature. I. Title.
  TL638.H53 2010
  797.5'1--dc22

                    2009008949

Printed in the USA

CG/CG

ROURKE PUBLISHING

www.rourkepublishing.com - rourke@rourkepublishing.com
Post Office Box 643328 Vero Beach, Florida 32964

TABLE OF CONTENTS

THINKING ABOUT
FLYING

Have you ever wondered about flying? Birds and bats flap their wings and glide through the skies effortlessly. Airplanes soar with tremendous speed and purpose. But a hot air balloon may be the most graceful way to fly through the air.

Many people celebrate special events, like anniversaries and birthdays, by taking a ride in a hot air balloon.

THE HISTORY OF

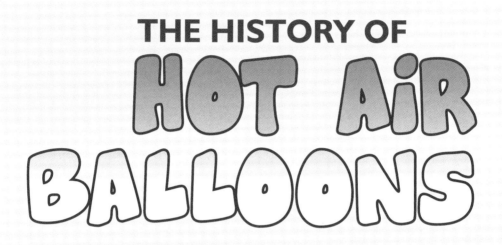

A young Frenchman named Joseph Montgolfier watched as the smoke and ash rose from a fire in his fireplace. Some historians say he thought about the floating clouds in the sky. Others would say his mind was focused on wanting to help the French military find a way to attack the enemy from the sky instead of on land.

Joseph Montgolfier

Joseph began to experiment with smoke and a paper bag. He and his brother Etienne thought that gas from the fire would fill the bag and cause it to rise. They called it **Montgolfier Gas**. The paper bags, though, kept catching on fire. By 1782, the brothers were using taffeta and other materials instead of the paper bag to hold the gas. Later, others discovered that it wasn't the gas or smoke, but it was the heat that caused the material to rise.

DID YOU KNOW?

Although the Montgolfier brothers receive credit for designing the first hot air balloons, the first recorded hot air balloon flight took place in Portugal on August 8, 1709. Father Bartolomeu de Gusmao set fire to twigs and sticks, and watched as his balloon rose to the ceiling of the royal palace, where it remained in the air for several seconds.

After many trials and experiments, on June 4, 1783, the Montgolfier brothers launched their first balloon to the delight of a large crowd in France. The balloon had a diameter of about 33 feet (10 meters) and traveled a distance of about 1 mile (1.6 kilometers).

Since that early launch, people still gather to enjoy the colorful display at balloon festivals. Albuquerque, New Mexico, hosts an International Balloon Festival every October, and Louisville, Kentucky, celebrates the sport with food, music, and hot air balloon races.

DID YOU KNOW?

The first living beings to travel as passengers in a hot air balloon were a sheep, a duck, and a rooster who traveled almost 2 miles (3.2 kilometers) in an 8-minute flight on September 19, 1783. All three animals landed safely.

THE PARTS OF THE BALLOON

Inventors experimented with different materials to make the balloons. Eventually, they discovered that **nylon** was the best material to use. Called the **envelope**, this fabric is the part of the balloon that fills with hot air. There is a layer of fire resistant material at the bottom of the envelope. This material is similar to the fabrics worn by race car drivers and firefighters.

The envelope of a hot air balloon displays a variety of bright colors and interesting patterns.

Inventors used different materials to lift early balloons into the air. They used wood, feathers, coal, paper, animal fats, and even whale oil to help the balloons get off the ground.

Today, a **burner** beneath the balloon produces a flame that reaches up into the bag and heats the air. The air inside the bag remains warmer than the surrounding air, and is therefore lighter than the outer air, which causes the bag to rise.

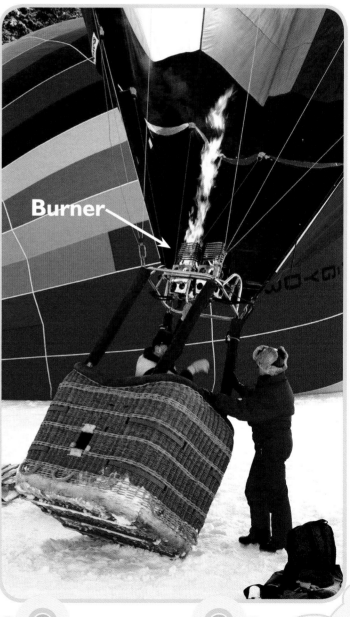

Burner

The pilot feeds fuel to the burner, which lifts the hot air balloon off the ground. To make the balloon rise higher, the pilot burns more fuel. To lose **altitude**, the pilot burns less fuel or opens the cooling vent to let out some of the warmer air. Once landed on the ground, the pilot pulls the **rip panel** to deflate the bag.

In order to fly a hot air balloon, a pilot must obtain a license from the Federal Aviation Administration and be at least 14 years old. A pilot has to be at least 16 years old to carry passengers.

Wicker Basket

The passengers ride in a basket that attaches to the balloon. Usually made of **wicker**, the basket needs to be strong enough to carry weight, but flexible enough to withstand repeated landings. The basket may be small to carry only a pilot, or large enough to carry fifteen people. The pilot uses thin cables, usually made of steel, to attach the basket to the envelope.

The **payload** consists of the basket, the equipment, the passengers, and the supplies. The heavier the payload, the larger the balloon must be to be able to lift off the ground. Balloon pilots have ground crews that follow each voyage to help with the landing.

USES FOR BALLOONS

Hot air balloons grew in importance during times of war. In the Civil War, World War I, and World War II, armies used balloons to observe the enemy and determine locations of oncoming troops. They also used **barrage balloons** to prevent low-flying enemy attacks. These captive balloons, held still with cables, would rip apart enemy planes that flew too low.

Hot air balloons are useful for research and science. Meteorologists use gas balloons equipped with an instrument called a **radiosonde** to measure temperature, humidity, pressure, and altitude.

Hot air balloon enthusiasts participate in races and rallies around the world almost every weekend. Some competitors participate in games. One game involves dropping bags of flour to try to hit a target. Some serious balloonists try to set records for traveling the fastest or longest distance. The United States National Championships are held annually. There is also a worldwide competition that takes place each fall with different countries serving as host.

Traveling in a hot air balloon is a great way to see the sights when visiting a new place, or explore while on vacation.

BALLOON FLIGHT

THROUGH THE YEARS

Timeline:

June 4, 1783:   The Montgolfier brothers launch their first balloon.

September 19, 1783:   A duck, a sheep, and a rooster are the first passengers to ride in a hot air balloon.

January 7, 1785:   Jean-Pierre Blanchard and Dr. John Jeffries are the first to fly across the English Channel.

1978:   Ben Abruzzo, Maxie Anderson, and Larry Newman are the first to cross the Atlantic Ocean.

1999:   Bertrand Piccard and Brian Jones are the first to fly around the world without landing, a flight of 25,361 miles (40,815 kilometers) in 19 days, 10 hours, and 24 minutes.

2002:   American Steve Fossett is the first to complete a solo trip around the world with an unofficial time of 13 days, 11 hours, and 33 minutes.

GLOSSARY

altitude (AL-ti-tood): the height of something above the ground

barrage balloons (buh-RAHZH buh-LOONZ): balloons, held captive by wires, used to prevent enemy attacks

burner (BUR-ner): a device used to produce heat or flame

envelope (EN-vuh-lope): the material of a hot air balloon, usually made of nylon

Montgolfier Gas (mont-GOL-fee-ur GASS): the name given to the gas that lifted the Montgolfier balloons, which was later found only to be heated air

nylon (NYE-lon): a strong synthetic fiber

payload (PAY-lohd): the load carried by a vehicle; including, in a balloon, those items necessary for its flight

radiosonde (RAY-dee-oh-sohnd): a miniature radio transmitter carried aloft, used to measure atmospheric conditions

rip panel (RIP PAN-uhl): a part of the balloon that allows air to be released from the envelope quickly

wicker (WIK-ur): thin, flexible twigs or branches, usually from a willow tree, used to make baskets and furniture

INDEX

WEBSITES TO VISIT

www.pbs.org/wgbh/nova/balloon

http://library.thinkquest.org/28629/page21.html

www.howstuffworks.com/hot-air-balloon.htm

www.pbskids.org/dragonflytv/show/balloon.html

www.hotairballoons/hot_air_balloon_facts.asp

http://pbskids.org/zoom/activities/sci/hotairballoon.html

ABOUT THE AUTHOR

Kelli Hicks grew up in Michigan and fondly remembers the beauty of the hot air balloon festivals that she and her family attended. She now lives in Florida with her husband and daughter, and still marvels at the sight of the beautiful balloons floating through the air.